SPIRITUAL DANCE

Fred,

For inspiration.

Leine Adamson

♡

SPIRITUAL DANCE

The Adamsone Method

Liene Adamsone

Library and Archives Canada Cataloguing in Publication

Adamsone, Liene, 1968–

    Spiritual dance : Adamsone method / Liene Adamsone.

ISBN 978-0-9811419-0-9

    1. Dance therapy. 2. Dance – Religious aspects. 3. Spiritual life. I. Title.

RC489.D3A33 2009   615.8'5155   C2009-907499-8

Editor: Judy Phillips
Design & production: Counterpunch Inc. / Peter Ross
Photography and illustration:
    Liene Adamsone: page 20
    Tatjana Brila, Fotolia.com: Jurmala, Latvia, page 76
    Gordon Hawkins: front cover, back cover, pages ii, 2, 6, 24, 31–69, 81, 88
    Ilze Viksnina: Baltic Sea / Latvia photos, pages 8, 10, 13, 14, 16, 73–75

Printed in Canada by Transcontinental Printers

For copies of this book, visit www.spiritualdance.ca

To my grandmother Olga Adamsone,

my inspiration and anchor throughout my life.

CONTENTS

Introduction   1

PART ONE   CONNECTING WITH YOUR INNER AND OUTER WORLDS   5

1   Learn to Love Your Body   7

2   Express Yourself through Dance   9

3   Connecting with Nature   11

4   The Energy Switch   15

5   Finding Balance   17

6   Unlocking Creativity in Children   21

7   Feeding Your Energy   25

PART TWO   THE SPIRITUAL DANCES   29

Chakras   30

Exercise 1   Energy Dance   32

Exercise 2   Chakra Balancing   38

Exercise 3   Energy Fountains   46

Exercise 4   Opening to the Universe   51

Exercise 5   Take and Give   58

Exercise 6   Becoming the Earth   62

Exercise 7   Time   66

Exercise 8   Four Elements   70

Exercise 9   Expressing Emotions   78

Epilogue   85

Acknowledgments   87

INTRODUCTION

To every question there is an answer: we just have to open ourselves up to let it in. For about four years I have wanted to write a book about dance. I believe that my dance philosophy, knowledge, and teaching experience will inspire many people to start dancing and to experience the incredible self-transformation that dance can bring. But every time I sat down to write, I didn't know how to begin. I had so much to say, but where to start? I could write easily in my diary about my day at the dance studio, my dreams and love that surround my work. My question was, how to put my dance philosophy that I use in my teaching down on paper?

It was July 8, 2007. I woke up early and started my day, as usual, with meditation and Kundalini yoga. That day my answer came to me through spiritual dance. As I was meditating and focusing on my chakras, letting energy flow through each, I had an empowering moment. It was as though someone had helped me get up off the floor and willed me to express the chakra exercise in dance form. I took off my clothes and let the information from the universe flow into my naked body. The energy flowed through my chakra centers and into my movements, creating a new dance form that connected my spirit

and body in sequenced motion. It was an incredibly powerful feeling. Many cultures have used some form of spiritual dance in various rituals, often to get rid of bad spirits. The spiritual dance that came to me from the universe and through my dance experiences takes the form of exercises that will help one let go of stress and negative emotion and bring healthy energy to the body. Anyone who practices these spiritual dance exercises will come to understand that we all possess everything we need to be able to dance.

That day, I received so much information from the universe that I was not sure that I would remember it all – I had to get a pen and paper, and this is how I began to write this book. In Part One I share with you some of the important influences in my life, including nature and children, and the impact they've had on my dance experience. I also explore the transformative nature of dance, and how it's available to each and every one of us. The section closes with a chapter on nutrition – necessary to fuel our bodies, energy, and spirit. In Part Two you'll find a brief explanation of chakras, followed by detailed descriptions of the spiritual dance exercises.

PART ONE

CONNECTING WITH YOUR INNER AND OUTER WORLDS

Think about your being – your physical body, your spirit – and about everything that surrounds you. Look up at the sky and imagine how far it goes. Although there seems to be no end to it, the beginning is you. Everything that's in you and around you makes you the way you are. In today's fast-paced world, we are forced to constantly adapt to changes around us. Letting our creativity blossom and expressing ourselves through movement can make a tremendous difference in our lives and help us deal with challenges, from the pressures of everyday life to ill health to emotional distress. We can unlock our creativity by becoming aware of our bodies, ourselves, and how we connect to the physical world around us and to the universe.

ONE

LEARN TO LOVE YOUR BODY

I used to dance naked in front of the mirror in the morning. Any emotions the music brought out I expressed through movement. Most of the movements had their base in ballet, since that's my profession and favorite form of dance, but it could have been any type of dance or even unstructured movement. As I did ballet jumps, my breasts had their own dance. While my body was moving through the air, my breasts were like an instrument in the orchestra, doing an original solo.

This naked morning dance helped me accept the changes my body went through during and after pregnancy. Many women have difficulty accepting such changes. Our breasts sag and we have stretch marks; our skin is looser and there is fat where before there was none. Letting dance take over your body is letting beauty flow in to every inch of it. Thanks to these dances, I learned to love my body, and I haven't wanted to change it since. I realized that what we think are imperfections or differences are the most beautiful parts of who we are: they make us unique.

Try dancing naked in front of a mirror. Look at your body with love; accept everything about it. Think about being a part of nature. Everything in nature is unique – no two trees are the same, but no matter how different they are, each radiates beauty. Accepting and loving yourself is what begins your connection with your inner spirit.

TWO

EXPRESS YOURSELF THROUGH DANCE

We all have what it takes to dance: the instrument of dance is the body. Dance is the expression of music or an emotion with our bodies. We can dance in silence or to sound. Some sounds we hear we may find unpleasant, like the sound of street traffic or construction, a vacuum or sewing machine. What if we imagine such sounds as the base of rhythm and dance to it? Find the dance rhythm in these sounds, then express your emotions – whatever you are feeling inside – through body movement, letting them out in a dance form. You will find that you undergo a transformation; your annoyance at the sound will dissipate as you express and release this emotion through dance.

We can also dance to the sounds of nature – to the sound of rain, wind, thunder, fire, water, birds, or rustling leaves. When we dance to these sounds, we become a part of nature and nature becomes a part of us. Nature has always been significant in my life and has helped shape my dance experience.

Using our bodies to express music or other sounds, or even silence, can be cathartic because it helps us release our emotions. Often, further, unexpected emotions arise as we continue to dance – continuing to express *those* feelings through movement can be therapeutic. In this way, dance contributes to our emotional well-being.

THREE

CONNECTING WITH NATURE

I grew up in Latvia near the Baltic Sea and spent every summer by the sea. To get to the water I had to walk through the woods, which in the early mornings was quiet. As I walked along the path, I would breathe in the aroma of the pine trees. The sound the trees made in the wind seemed to whisper to me, saying, "Come to me, feel me." And I did. I wrapped my arms around a tree and pressed my body against it, my lips touching the rough bark of the trunk. I could feel the life in the tree. Hugging and kissing it made me feel connected with both the past and the future – the tree had already seen so much, having stood there for years, since long before I was born, and it likely would continue to stand there once I was gone. Every time I walked through the woods I wanted to hug the trees and feel their energy, and if there was no one else around, I did.

At the shore, as I walked on the golden beach, I felt energy coming through my bare feet from the sand. The feeling wasn't always the same. Sometimes when heated by the sun, the sand almost burned my feet. After a rain shower it sometimes felt rough, and sometimes it felt soft, like silk or velvet.

The most empowering and changing energy I felt came from the sea. The Baltic Sea is usually cold, and I had to walk very far out from the shoreline to get to water deep enough to swim in. Each of the feelings I got from the water are memorable. On those rare days when the water was very warm, I felt as though I had an instant connection to it. When it was cold, I felt an unwelcomeness as I waded in the shallow water. But once I was far enough out to swim, there was nothing else – just me and the sea. Even though I was a very small part in the big sea, I felt connected to it.

My connection with the Baltic Sea became so strong that I began swimming in it even during winter, when the water was freezing cold. I always felt energized afterward, and my immune system became very strong. When I was nineteen and working in the theater as a ballerina, I could not resist stopping by the sea for a swim before going home on nights after a performance. At night the sea became more mysterious, and swimming in the dark, guided only by the moon and stars, was incredible. On those nights I felt like I was making love with the sea. It wasn't just me being a part of nature; the sea became a part of me. I felt safe and connected to it. Some nights it was completely dark, with no stars visible in the sky, and the waves just carried me along.

My connection with the sea at night opened up in me a trust in nature and made me incredibly passionate about my physical connection with it – swimming naked in the sea, feeling the tree bark with my lips. This passion gave me much courage in life. Nothing could stop me from going on my night swims in the sea. Once, I told my husband that on my way home, at around midnight, I had stopped for a swim. He begged me not to do it again because it was dangerous. And even though he was probably right, I could not give up my swims.

Growing up by the sea and the woods allowed me to feel connected with nature, and experiencing nature through different moods of the

weather allowed me to feel different energies from nature.
Now, I express my connection with nature in my choreography
and dance therapy.

What part of nature do you feel most connected with? The ocean,
the mountains, the woods? Next time you are surrounded by nature,
visualize that you are a part of it. Feel the energy, breathe in the scents,
take it all in to your body. If there is a safe place outdoors where you
feel comfortable, perhaps near water or in the woods, try expressing
your connection to nature through movement. Movement changes
your mood, and it will make you feel even more connected to nature's
powerful energy. (Have you ever tried dancing in the warm summer
rain?) The Four Elements exercise in Part Two is a good introduction
to exploring our connection to nature's elements – water, air, earth,
and fire.

FOUR

THE ENERGY SWITCH

We are surrounded with energy from the universe; it is floating around us, and coming from the things around us – the earth, the air, the rocks, the trees. When you feel emotionally empty and low on energy, just remember all this energy surrounding you. Open yourself up and let it in. Once the energy has entered your body, the switch happens: you feel more energized and have an increased sense of well-being.

The mind is an important instrument in this switch. If you continue to think how tired you are and what hurts, you are blocking the channels through which energy enters your body. The first step is to start thinking positively. Think about all the good energy that is surrounding you. You can imagine this energy in any form. For instance, imagine that birds are flying around you, holding beautiful flowers in their beaks. They brought these flowers to you from far away and want to give them to you, but you don't see them. Open up your imagination and see these birds, let them come and give the flowers to you. Let the energy in and feel the switch.

FIVE

FINDING BALANCE

The word *balance* has many meanings. Having balance in life means doing what you have to do and also what you want to do – for example, giving time both to your important responsibilities, such as work and family, and to your personal goals. It also means not focusing on one activity, no matter how much you may love it, to the exclusion of all others.

Finding balance in life can be very difficult, but it's easier to do when you know the purpose of your life. Even if you love your work and taking care of your family, it's important to also figure out what your personal goals are, and to then devote time and energy to them. Doing things you love to do and working toward your personal goals will give you a feeling of fulfillment, so that at the end of the day you don't feel empty. If you balance your time by including some enjoyable personal activity every day, you will find it easier to do those activities that are less enjoyable – even chores like grocery shopping.

What will bring more balance and joy to your day?

For me, I know that if I have a good night's sleep – eight to ten hours – I will be productive in everything I do the next day. Starting my day with meditation, even if for only five minutes, makes a difference. I find the breathing exercises and mind focus very calming.

During the day, whenever I feel rushed, I take a deep breath and thank my angels for their hard work, and the universe for all its teachings, for my life and the people in it, and for everything that surrounds me. Every day I find time to have a conversation with my daughter, to eat nutritiously, and to take a bubble bath. These things help me feel balanced in life and get me through those activities that I have to do but don't particularly enjoy.

In dance, balance is being able to remain in one position – a relevé, retiré, arabesque, or attitude, for example – for a length of time. Doing so requires you to have focus and control of your body. Not only does your mind need to be completely focused on the position you are in, but you also must be able to control that position by being aware of every inch of your body. As soon as you let other thoughts enter your mind, you'll start to lose the balance. For instance, if you begin thinking about something upsetting that happened that day, you will find that it is difficult to keep your balance. Thoughts are like wind: they can disturb your stillness. To achieve balance in dance, you have to be right there, right then, focused on the position you are holding and only on that position. To be able to do this, you need to believe in yourself. Your body is the instrument of dance. Your mind directs this instrument. By focusing you will achieve the poses and movements you are striving for.

Before you take any given position, visualize the position, and then visualize yourself in the position. By "visualize" I mean have a snapshot in your mind of how the pose is supposed to look or, if the teacher is demonstrating the movement, capture a picture of it in your mind and then visualize yourself in the same position.

When you truly dance, everything that has occurred or will occur seems not to exist: it is just you there right then in the moment. And when you are focused on and balanced in the moment, your body is the instrument of a beautiful art form. You will feel the joy in accomplishing this. Your mind may try to get the better of you, but just remember, your thoughts are like wind. If you allow them in, you will lose your focus and balance. Let the wind pass by without touching you.

SIX

UNLOCKING CREATIVITY IN CHILDREN

Working with children is one of the biggest gifts in my life. I have learned so much from every one of them. My youngest student is two years old. At her first lesson, even though she couldn't yet talk, she followed everything I and the other students did. Many children dance before they can talk. My mother told me that when I was just an infant, she would lift me up in the air and I would move my legs as though I were dancing – I was dancing before I could talk or walk.

We are all individuals, and children, especially at a young age, express this in everything they do. When we come into this world and have our parents to take care of us, we feel safe. We can just be who we are and express the way we feel without reservation.

In September 2007, at the beginning of a new season at the dance studio, I drew a picture of ballerinas, each wearing a different costume. As I colored the picture I thought, what a gift it would be if these ballerinas came to me. That same day, the gift arrived: twelve girls came to the class for four to six year olds. It was my biggest class that season.

A different approach is needed with every child. At this young age, children are very honest, and their character shows in everything they do. Before we start class, each student chooses a toy to place beside the barre and to dance with later. While the children are choosing their toys, I talk to them and observe their behavior. Some know right away which toy to pick, while others have a difficult time choosing; these ones I help make a decision. One girl always wants the frog toy and becomes sad if someone else takes it. Another girl always says that she doesn't want a toy and doesn't take one. I allow that and encourage her to pick a toy later, when we dance with them.

Once the children have put their toys beside the barre, we sit in a circle on the floor, with the soles of our feet touching, to do a stretching exercise called Pizza – together in a circle we make up the pizza pie. Stretching forward, first we make the "dough" with our hands, then "spread" on the "tomato sauce." Then we "grate" the "cheese" and sprinkle it on top. I remind the children to reach to the middle of the pizza; this will be the deepest stretch. Next, we choose the pizza toppings, and here again the individuality and character of each child comes out. When I ask, "What would you like on your pizza?" some of the children answer right away – they can't wait to tell me what toppings they want. Others, though, don't say anything. So then I ask the same question a different way. If I know a student is shy, I ask, "Would you like tomatoes, mushrooms, or peppers on your pizza?" And the student is happy to answer "tomatoes." If I simply repeated the original question, some of the students would remain silent, and I would be able to see sadness in their eyes, maybe even fear and confusion because they are shy and not used to speaking up in a group.

By approaching each child in a way appropriate for her or him, I instill confidence and trust in the children, and they learn that they don't need to be afraid. In this way we develop a closeness, which allows the children to open up and be creative in dance. After about six months of doing dance once or twice a week, the shy girl is happy and anxious to tell me what toppings she wants on her pizza. And the girl who didn't want a toy now has found her favorite teddy bear.

There are other excellent dance exercises for unlocking children's creativity. In the Animal dance we pretend to be giraffes, tigers, birds, butterflies, snakes, and fish. Then I might suggest the children show the difference between, say, a snake and a fish. This prompts them to be even more creative: How can the body show this difference when these two animal movements are so similar? The most difficult part of the exercise is portraying an animal without making any sounds. It's easy to express a dog by barking and a cat by meowing, a bird by chirping, and a snake by hissing. It becomes much harder if the only instrument is the body. Sometimes I let the students choose which animal they'll pretend to be. If I can't guess what they are, I ask them, and often I hear names I've never heard before – I'm not sure if such animals even exist.

Young children have so much interest in – and innate knowledge of – the world. When they are able to express that in dance, their creativity opens up, and when I see them smiling, I can sense that they are happy. Once you've felt this creativity and happiness through dance, the feelings brought about by unnatural means will never compare. The happiness that comes from dance stays with you all your life. For me, it overrides any interest in drugs or alcohol. I call this happiness being high on life. I am sure that many of my students will continue to dance throughout their lives, because the happiness that comes from it opens up a new world of expression and creative ability, no matter how shy they are.

This talent is in every one of us – we just have to connect to it. It's never too late. Just remember that each of us is unique and no single approach works for everyone. Through experimentation, you'll find the approach that is right for you to let go and believe in yourself.

SEVEN

FEEDING YOUR ENERGY

There is a saying "We are what we eat," and if you think about it, that makes a lot of sense. The food we put in our mouth affects our entire system. We can purify ourselves from the outside, taking good care of our skin, hair, and nails. We can do the same on the inside, through the foods we choose to eat. Just as putting chemicals and other unhealthy products on our skin or hair is not good for us, putting processed foods filled with chemicals and stripped of their nutrients into our bodies is detrimental to our health.

When selecting food, choose whole grains, proteins (meat in small portions, poultry, seafood, and legumes), vegetables, fruit, and water. These choices are whole foods that together offer the vitamins, minerals, and other nutrients our body needs. Limit or avoid soda pop, chips, and foods made with refined flour and sugar or containing trans fats. The refining process strips foods of their nutrients, and those made with sugar and trans fats are known to be bad for us or at the very least don't offer our bodies any nourishment. Keeping a food journal in which you record what and how much you eat and drink each day for a week will allow you to easily see what food choices you make, and where you might want to make changes.

Each of us is unique, and every person needs to find his or her own way to stay healthy and happy. Just as some of us feel refreshed after sleeping for only six hours while others need eight to ten hours of sleep, some of us choose to be vegetarians or vegans, while others feel they need to eat meat. Over the years I have learned what works for me. My day typically starts with a cup of coffee and a bowl of old-fashioned oatmeal. At around noon I have freshly squeezed vegetable juice. In winter, instead of juice I make gingerroot tea. For lunch, at around one o'clock, I eat red meat, poultry, or seafood with vegetables and potatoes or yams. At around three o'clock I have a whole-grain sandwich with tomatoes, cucumber, or spinach, and leftovers from lunch. For dinner I like to make soup. My favorites are borsch and chicken soup. I always bring fruit and water with me to work. Once in a while I treat myself to a Starbucks oatmeal raisin cookie.

It's important to allow yourself to indulge in a treat. If you know that the treat is coming, it will be easier to choose healthy foods more often. Treat yourself, whether it be to ice cream, chocolate, or whatever else you like, on a day when you do more physical activity than usual. The key is to know that the treat is coming – just not every day.

Here are my tips for healthy eating:

* Learn how to select the best foods for your health.
* Learn what foods to limit or avoid.
* Eat breakfast every day – it will kick-start your metabolism.
* Allow yourself your favorite treat – not every day, but perhaps once a week or so.
* Drink at least six cups of water each day.
* Take a healthy snack – apples or carrots, for example – with you to work or if you will be away from home for any length of time.
* Don't eat less than two hours before going to bed. Eating too close to sleep time may result in poor sleep, since your body is working hard to digest and process the food.

Health is the most important thing in life, and it can be very difficult to enjoy the things life has to offer when you get sick. Eating well will help ensure you stay healthy, or recover quickly from an injury or illness. It fuels our energy, which we need for a healthy body and spirit.

PART TWO

THE SPIRITUAL DANCES

In the spiritual dances, energy flows through the body's chakra centers and into your movements to connect body, mind, and spirit. These dances take the form of exercises that are meant to promote balance of the body's chakras and foster harmony among them, improving your well-being. They will help you let go of stress and negative emotion and bring healthy energy to your body. By calling on you to access your emotions and express them through dance, these exercises will also awaken your creativity.

CHAKRAS

The body has seven chakras, or energy centers. *Chakra* is a Sanskrit word meaning wheel or circle. Chakras are thought to funnel spiritual energy into the body, bringing vitality to the organs. They are located in precise places in the body, beginning at the base of the spinal column and moving upward to the top of the head, close to the major endocrine organs, those organs that secrete directly into the blood. Each chakra is associated with the health of particular organs, as well as with various emotions and behaviors. An imbalance in your chakras might manifest itself in various ways, spiritually or physically; focusing on a particular chakra allows you to work on the health, emotions, and behaviors associated with that chakra.

As you can see from the list on page 31, each chakra also has an associated element, such as earth or fire, and associated colors. As well, each chakra is fueled by particular foods. The list here is by no means exhaustive. Lots of literature is widely available on these energy centers. My favorite book on the topic is *Tantric Awakening*, by Valerie Brooks.

The Seven Chakras

1. Root Chakra
Location: base of the spine
Color: red
Element: earth
Organs: adrenal glands
Governs: survival, security, safety, confidence
Dysfunctions: anxiety, tension, restlessness, constipation
Food: root vegetables, protein-rich foods

2. Navel Chakra
Location: about two inches below the navel
Color: orange
Element: water
Organs: sex glands
Governs: nurturing, sexuality, sensuality
Dysfunctions: lack of passion, mood swings, sexual dysfunction, loss of appetite
Food: sweet fruits, almonds, honey

3. Solar Plexus Chakra
Location: solar plexus
Color: yellow
Element: fire
Organs: pancreas, liver, spleen, digestive tract
Governs: willpower, self-esteem
Dysfunctions: low energy, low self-esteem, hypertension
Food: grains, seeds, ginger, dairy products

4. Heart Chakra
Location: heart
Color: green
Element: air
Organs: heart, lungs, circulatory system, thymus glands
Governs: love, relationships
Dysfunctions: loneliness, depression, chest pain, high blood pressure
Foods: spinach, kale, broccoli, cauliflower, cabbage, celery

5. Throat Chakra
Location: throat
Color: light blue
Element: ether
Organs: thyroid glands, throat
Governs: communication, self-expression
Dysfunctions: difficulty expressing oneself, disorders of the throat
Food: water, fruit juices, herbal teas

6. Third Eye Chakra
Location: center of the forehead
Color: indigo
Element: light
Organs: pituitary gland, hypothalamus
Governs: intuition, imagination
Dysfunctions: lack of imagination, headaches
Food: red grapes, berries

7. Crown Chakra
Location: top of the head
Color: violet
Element: cosmic energy
Organs: pineal gland, endocrine system
Governs: spirituality, connection with the universe
Dysfunctions: greed, migraines
Food: fasting

ENERGY DANCE

I like to do the energy dance early in the morning as the sun is rising. As I face the window in my room, the light streaming in, I can feel the fresh air entering through the open window, and the rhythm of the music asks my body to start moving. Choose the time and place that is right for you.

This dance can be done to any music you like so long as it has a definite rhythm. My favorite music is from the album *Sunset and Sunrise* by Greek DJ Alexandros Christopoulos. If you are outside, surrounded by nature, you can dance to the sound of nature – for instance, the rustling of trees or the pounding of waves. Or you may wish to dance in silence.

Standing with your feet hip-width apart,
close your eyes and concentrate on your
seven energy centers, one by one. Visualize
your chakras as blossoming flowers, each
a different color (see page 31) that radiates
energy.

Open your eyes and let the rhythm of the
music flow into your body. Place your
palms together, with your fingers pointing
downward at your root chakra (1). Slowly
bring your hands up to your navel chakra
and then to your solar plexus chakra (2).

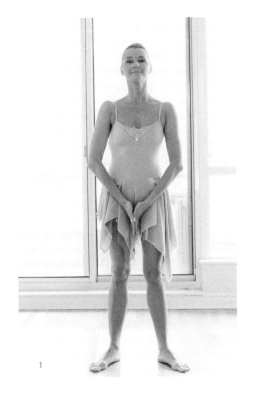

1

2

3

4

Rotate your fingers so they are pointing upward (3). Bring your hands to your heart chakra, then your throat chakra, then your third eye chakra, and, finally, your crown chakra (4–7). As you do this, visualize energy as a bright light coming from the earth, entering your body through your root chakra and traveling through each energy center all the way to your crown chakra.

Stretch your arms above your head, keeping your hands together, fingers still pointing upward, to release the energy into the universe (8).

5

6

7

8

9

10

Now switch the direction. Keeping your palms together, fingers pointing upward, visualize the energy of the universe as a bright light coming into your body through your crown chakra and flowing through each chakra as you slowly draw your hands downward (9–12).

When you reach your solar plexus chakra, rotate your fingers so they are pointing toward the ground (13), and continue drawing your hands downward so that the energy is moving through your root chakra and into the earth (14).

Repeat several times.

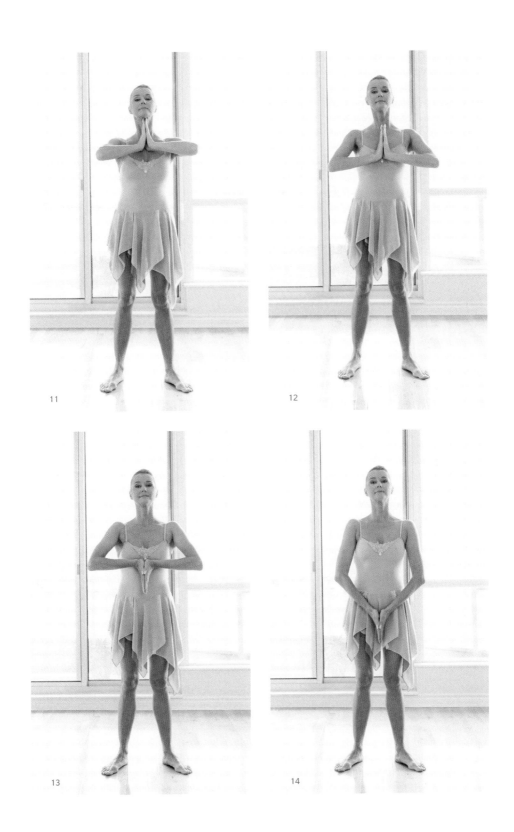

11

12

13

14

CHAKRA BALANCING

This series of exercises will help you determine if any of your energy centers are blocked or out of balance. Pay attention to the sensations in each of your chakras while doing the exercise. You may feel heat in the chakra areas and in your hands; this is the energy coming from the chakras. If you feel any discomfort (such as pressure) in these areas, it may mean that the chakras are blocked. Notice in which area you feel discomfort, and note which organs and qualities (e.g., self-esteem, confidence) are governed by that particular chakra.

This series of exercises is done with your eyes open, your gaze focused on one spot ahead of you at eye level. Do the series in a continuous motion, flowing from one exercise to the next.

After completing all of the positions with the right foot off the floor, repeat the exercises, this time with your left foot off the floor, and with your right hand on top of the left for the navel, solar plexus, heart, throat, and third eye chakra exercises.

Root Chakra

Imagine your root chakra blossoming like a red flower. With your palms together and fingers clasped, hold your hands near your root chakra. Bending the right knee, lift your right foot slightly off the floor. Find the position of your body that allows you to stand with all your weight on your left foot without moving. You may wish to touch your left foot with the toes of your right foot, as demonstrated in the photo. Hold this position for 30 seconds, breathing deeply.

Navel Chakra

Imagine your navel chakra blossoming like an orange flower. Place your right palm on your abdomen below your belly button and then your left hand on top of the right. Raise your right foot slightly, pointing your foot so that the big toe is touching your left ankle, as demonstrated in the photo. Hold this position for 30 seconds, breathing deeply.

Solar Plexus Chakra

Imagine your solar plexus chakra
blossoming like a yellow flower.
Place your right palm over your
solar plexus chakra and then your
left hand on top of the right. Draw
your right foot up your leg, so that
the big toe is touching your left
calf, as demonstrated in the photo.
Hold this position for 30 seconds,
breathing deeply.

Heart Chakra

Imagine your heart chakra blossoming like a green flower. Place your right palm over your heart chakra and then your left hand on top of the right hand. Draw your right foot higher up the left leg, so that the big toe is touching your left leg just below the knee, as demonstrated in the photo. Hold this position for 30 seconds, breathing deeply.

Throat Chakra

Imagine your throat chakra
blossoming like a light blue flower.
Place your right palm on your
throat and then your left hand on
top of the right. Draw your right
foot up your left leg so that the big
toe is touching your left leg just
above the knee, as demonstrated
in the photo. Hold this position for
30 seconds, breathing deeply.

Third Eye Chakra

Imagine your third eye chakra blossoming like an indigo-colored flower. Place your right palm on the top of your forehead and then your left hand on top of the right. Raise your right foot off the floor so that the sole of the foot is pressed against your left inner thigh, as demonstrated in the photo. Hold this position for 30 seconds, breathing deeply.

Crown Chakra

Imagine a violet flower blossoming from your crown chakra toward the sky. With your feet hip-width apart and your arms stretched above your head, stand on your tiptoes, as demonstrated in the photo. If you find it too difficult to stay balanced on your tiptoes, stand with your feet apart and flat on the floor. Hold this position for 30 seconds, breathing deeply.

Now repeat the series of exercises on the other side.

ENERGY FOUNTAINS

In this series of exercises your body will be a channel for the energy that comes from the earth and universe. Visualizing the energy flowing through your chakras and coming out of your body like a fountain will help you feel energized and purified. Once you are familiar with the exercises, you can flow from one to the other in a continuous motion.

Toward the Universe

Stand with your feet together, arms stretched straight above your head, palms parallel to each other. With your eyes closed, visualize the energy as a bright light coming up from the earth into your body, flowing through your root chakra and then through the other chakras as it moves upward through your crown chakra and into the universe. Hold this position for 1 minute.

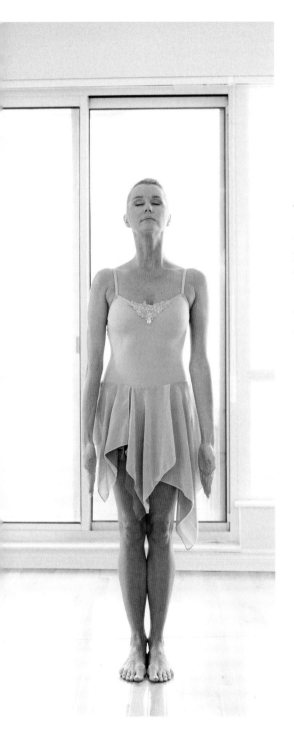

Toward the Earth

Stand with your feet together, your arms at your sides. With your eyes closed, visualize the energy as a bright light coming from the universe through your crown chakra and flowing downward through each chakra to the root chakra and finally into the earth. Hold this position for 1 minute.

Energy Fountain into the Universe

Standing with your feet hip-width apart,
open your arms wide above your head in
a V shape. With your eyes closed, visualize
the energy as a bright light coming from
the earth into your body through your
root chakra, flowing upward through
each chakra to your crown chakra, and
then into the universe as if in a fountain
as it exits the crown chakra. Hold this
position for 1 minute.

Energy Fountain into the Earth

Stand with your feet hip-width apart, your arms held in an upside-down V at your sides. With your eyes closed, visualize the energy as a bright light coming from the universe into your body through your crown chakra and then flowing downward through each chakra to the root chakra and, finally, into the earth as if in a fountain. Hold this position for 1 minute.

OPENING TO THE UNIVERSE

This series of exercises will help you feel the source of life. Imagine a very small, dry, flower seed. The seed is planted and starts to grow, producing a bud and, finally, a blossoming flower that radiates color and life. In these exercises, your hands represent the seed, the bud, and the flower. The type of flower and the color you visualize doesn't matter – visualize any you like.

1

2

Seed

Standing with your feet hip-width apart, stretch your arms above your head, holding your hands together with fingers clasped (1). Visualize your hands as a flower seed. Slowly move your arms and upper body in a circular motion, in whichever direction feels most natural to you, with your hands still together above your head (2–7). You may want to bend your knees as your arms circle downward and you bend forward, straightening them again as your arms reach toward the sky.

Do this movement for 1 minute, increasing the range of the circular motion as you move through the exercise.

5

3

4

6

7

1

2

Bud

Keeping your feet apart, stretch your arms above your head, palms together, fingers pointing upward (1). Visualize your hands as a flower bud. Slowly move your arms and upper body in a circular motion, in whichever direction feels most natural to you, with your hands still together above your head (2–7). You may want to bend your knees as you circle forward, straightening them again as your arms reach toward the sky.

Do this movement for 1 minute, increasing the range of the circular motion as you move through the exercise.

5

3

4

6

7

1

2

Flower

Slowly open your hands and arms into a V shape above your head (1). Visualize your hands as a blossoming flower. Slowly move your arms and upper body in a circular motion, in whichever direction feels most natural to you (2–6). You may want to bend your knees as you circle forward. Feel the energy from the flower going into the universe.

Do this movement for 1 minute, increasing the range of the circular motion as you move through the exercise.

TAKE AND GIVE

In this exercise, energy flows in a horizontal direction and through your heart chakra. As you do the exercise, think about acts of kindness – instances when people have been nice to you. It might be something as simple as someone holding the door open for you when your hands were full. Chances are that you felt like reciprocating by being kind to another person, maybe just smiling and wishing a stranger a good day. This exercise is about accepting the energy and then giving it away.

This exercise has a pull-push feel to it. Turn toward your right side, your right leg bent in plié position, the knee aligned with the toes. Extend your left leg behind you, so you're in a slight lunge.

From the right side, pull with your hands toward you (1). It may help to imagine that you are pulling a rope with a heavy object, say, a glowing bundle of light, tied at the end. Do this motion for at least 15 seconds.

Once the "object" has reached you, turn to the left side and, standing in a slight lunge, your left leg in front, push the object away, for at least 15 seconds (2).

Continue to pull from the right and push to the left for a total of 2 minutes.

3

Now switch directions of the exercise.
Begin facing the left, with your left leg bent
in a slight lunge position in front of you.
Pull from the left side for 15 seconds, then turn
and push toward the right for 15 seconds (3).

4

Continue to pull from the left and push to the
right for a total of 2 minutes (4).

BECOMING THE EARTH

In this exercise, energy flows in a horizontal direction. While doing the exercise, think about your body becoming one with the earth.

Stand upright with your arms at your sides (1). Turn toward your right side and lean over, stretching out your hands, arms, torso, and left leg so that they are parallel to the ground, your left foot pointed or flexed. Your right leg, which is your supporting leg, is in plié position, the knee bent and aligned with the toes (2).

Stretch out in this position, called the earth position, for a few moments, then return to the starting position.

Now switch the side and direction of the stretch. Feel as though your hands, arms, head, torso, and raised leg are the surface of the earth (3). Repeat this exercise several times, for up to 2 minutes.

To finish, lie on the floor and feel your body
connecting to the earth, with all of your
matter becoming part of the earth (4).

TIME

In this exercise, you "become" time. Whether time goes by slowly or quickly, what really matters is the present moment. When you are wholly in the present moment, the "speed" of time becomes irrelevant. Each new second is the present moment: you are in the now.

Standing with your feet hip-width apart,
stretch out your arms to the sides (1).
Circle your right arm clockwise in fairly rigid
movements, like the ticking second hand of
a clock (2–5).

Do this for 30 seconds or so, about 4 or 5
full rotations (see page 69).

Now begin to circle your right arm faster and then faster still, for 15 seconds.

Switch arms, circling your left arm counter-clockwise in fairly rigid movements, like the ticking second hand of a clock. Now move your left arm faster and faster, for 15 seconds.

Finish by circling your right arm clockwise as you circle your left arm counter-clockwise, in alternating sequence (when your right hand is at "6 o'clock," your left hand will be at around "12 o'clock," and vice-versa). Do this movement as fast as you can, for about 20 seconds.

To finish, stretch out your arms to the side and breathe deeply.

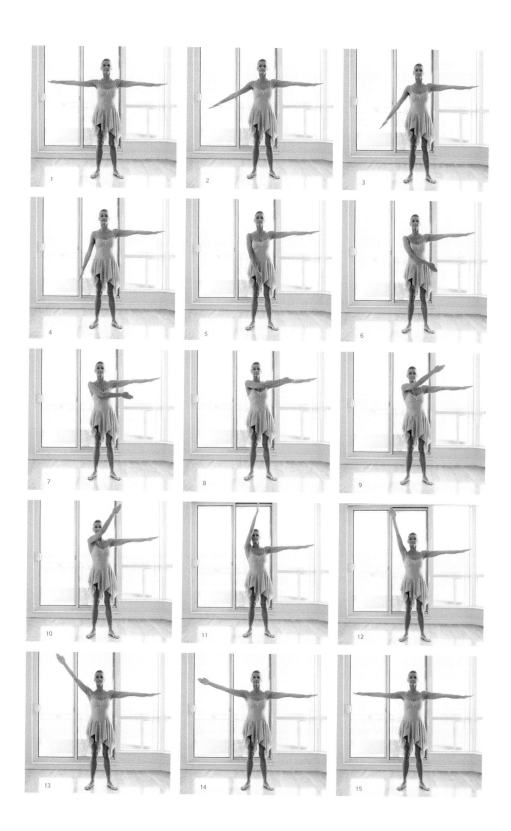

FOUR ELEMENTS

This series of exercises is about connecting with the four classical elements of the universe: water, air, earth, and fire. The objective is to first experience being a part of each of these elements, then to feel all four elements being a part of you. These exercises will help you feel purified and energized. They don't call for specific movements; just let your body express your feelings through movement in any way you like.

Be a Part of the Elements

Create a location for each of these elements. Let's say that water is in front of you – you might imagine it as a sea or an ocean, or a river. To your right is air – you might imagine it as mountains, their peaks enveloped in clouds. On your left is the earth – you might imagine it as the woods, with various types of trees, and fields. And, finally, behind you is fire – this you might visualize as the sun high up in the sky, shining brightly.

To connect with the element, move toward it, touching it with your hands, letting it into your body. How did you feel last time you swam in the ocean? When up in the mountains, or in the woods, feeling the heat of the sun? Let these feelings out in the form of improvised dance.

Water

Take a few steps forward, visualizing the water in front of you. Touch it with your hands. Perhaps you feel like jumping in and swimming, or just lying down in the shallow water and feeling its wetness on your body. Express this connection with water through body movement, for 30 seconds. I like to pretend I splash the water all over my body and then dive in and swim under the water, observing what kind of life is there.

Air

Next, connect with air, which is to your right. Take a few steps toward the right and imagine being on top of a mountain. Feel the pure air, breathe deeply, reach out and touch the clouds. Express this connection with air through body movement, for 30 seconds. I like to pretend I am grabbing the thin air with my hands, but it is transparent and I can't hold on to it – I can only breathe in and feel my lungs being purified.

Earth

Now connect with the earth, which is to your left. Take a few steps toward the left and imagine you are entering the woods, with its big, old trees. You find a field where you can lie down and smell the grass, touch the ground, feel the soil slipping through your fingers. Express your connection with the earth through body movement, for 30 seconds. I like to pretend that I am touching the soil with my hands; then I lie down in the field and feel the ground, as in the Becoming the Earth exercise (see page 65).

Fire

Now turn around and take a few steps toward the fire, which is behind you. Feel the heat coming from the sun: it's as hot as flames and you would like to touch it, but it burns your fingers, so you keep your distance, still able to feel the heat. Express your connection with fire through body movement, for 30 seconds. I like to reach up to try to touch the fire with my fingers, feeling the burning sensation on my hands. I feel the sun's hot rays coming toward me, and I let the heat into my body.

Let the Elements Be a Part of You

Now, express the four elements, in turn,
as though you are them.

Water

First you are water. Take a few steps forward
to where the water is and "become" this
element. For example, you might express
being the water by lying down and making
wave-like movements with your body.
Move in any way you feel like to be the
water. Do this for 30 seconds.

Air

Now you are going to be air. Take a few steps
toward the right and dance as though you are
pure air in, say, the mountains. You might
make slow movements, like a cloud moving
in the wind. Express being the element of air
in any way you like, for 30 seconds.

Earth

Now you are going to be the earth. Take a
few steps toward the left and express with
your body the feeling of being the earth,
for 30 seconds. You can do this by lying
down, as in the Becoming the Earth exercise
(see page 65), or in any way you like.

Fire

Next you are going to be fire. Turn around and take a few steps toward the fire, which is behind you. Dance as though you are the sun, for 30 seconds. You might express the sun's rays with arm movements, or dance in any way you feel like expressing being the sun.

To Be Complete

To finish, dance as if the four elements are in you, a part of you. You might repeat the movements you did when you were connecting to the elements – when you were a part of the elements – but this time imagine the water, air, earth, and fire being inside you. Dance with energy and a feeling of being complete. Dance in any way you are moved to. At this part of the exercise I like to let go and do any movements that my body feels like doing. Sometimes I jump, other times I run around the room as I move my arms. This part of the exercise is a great opportunity for improvisation and expression of your spirit.

After completing the series of exercises, it is a good idea to sit down comfortably on the floor and breathe deeply. You may still feel like you are one of the four elements. Sit quietly, closing your eyes if you like, and absorb your feelings. It always takes me a couple of minutes to see the room I'm in as being just a room. When I do these exercises, I let go of reality – I truly believe I am in nature. The connection I have had with nature throughout my life helps me create the feeling of being in it, no matter where I am.

EXPRESSING EMOTIONS

What is your overriding emotion today? How do you feel? What is your spirit telling you? Sometimes for no apparent reason we wake up happy, energized, and feeling surrounded by love. Other days we feel sad, tired, irritated, or indifferent. Despite this, each day we experience many emotions. Pay attention to them and bring them out through the spiritual dance exercises. In "Express Yourself through Dance," on page 9, I talk about expressing sounds (or even silence), and the emotions that arise from hearing these sounds, with your body. This series of exercises focuses on expressing emotions. In my spiritual dance class, I ask the students, what was the strongest emotion of your week? Then we dance, expressing one or two of these emotions by letting it go through movement, letting our spirits guide us. As in the Four Element exercises, these exercises don't call for any specific movements; just let your body express the feeling through movement in any way you like.

Lonely

Let this emotion out through dance; let your spirit guide you, expressing this emotion with any movements you like. I like to imagine being in a big cocoon, then breaking through the walls of this cocoon and seeing the four elements around me in the form of nature: the ocean, mountains, woods, and sun, as in the Four Elements exercises (see page 70). I express my being lonely with movements connected to nature – pretending to splash water on myself, taking long steps into the mountains, breathing deeply as I feel the fresh air enter my lungs, running into the woods, touching the ground, feeling the soil between my fingers, stretching out my arms toward the sun and feeling its heat.

Connecting with the four elements, I let my loneliness be part of nature by imagining that I am a drop of water in the ocean, knowing that the ocean could not exist without all the single drops of water together. By expressing my emotion with these movements, my feeling of loneliness transitions into a feeling of connection and belonging.

Sad

Let this emotion out through dance; let your spirit guide you, expressing this emotion with any movements you like. Typically, sadness calls for slow movement. I often imagine being in the rain, all the raindrops being the tears of nature crying for my sadness. I let the rain comfort me, let them soak my face, hair, clothes. I take slow, long steps, and reach up with my hands to feel nature's tears. Sometimes in this exercise we connect with the emotion of sadness so deeply that it brings out our own tears. Don't hold back – just let them out.

Angry, Frustrated

Let these emotions out through dance; let your spirit guide you, expressing these emotions with any movements you like. In class, we sometimes express anger and frustration by dancing like tigers. First we start as kittens, then we grow bigger, eventually "becoming" angry, hungry tigers.

We make our hands look like paws by spreading our fingers, and move as though we were tigers, crawling, running, and jumping, hunting for food. This is the only exercise in which we use our voices, roaring as loud as we can. If you try this, you'll see that it is not easy to make a sound like a tiger. We do this several times, and I often have to encourage, "Louder! Louder!"

Happy

Let this emotion out through dance; let your spirit guide you, expressing this emotion with any movements you like. Typically, happiness asks for fast movement, often jumping. For instance, if I am at home, my favorite way to express this emotion is by jumping on the bed like a little kid. When I do that I feel as though all my happiness is jumping with me and filling the room. In the dance studio we use the space to jump and run and reach out our arms in expression of this emotion.

Love

Let this emotion out through dance, let your spirit guide you, expressing this emotion with any movements you like. Love is around us in everything we see and do. Pure love is innocent and fragile like a flower just about to bloom. It is an incredible source of life and energy. When we do things with love, we create more energy around us.

Expressing love through dance, I like to imagine being a small flower growing under a large tree and, as I start blooming, I look up to see the powerful tree looking down at me. The tree is very happy to see me reaching up, growing toward its branches. I fall in love with this tree, and its powerful energy makes me grow taller. The tree is reaching down with its big branches and I know that one day we will finally connect.

There are many ways to express your feelings and emotions with dance movement, just use your imagination, perhaps even creating a story like mine of the flower and tree. It is a good idea to finish this series of exercises with the expression of a positive emotion, such as happiness or love.

EPILOGUE

We are all individuals, leading varied lives. There is no other person like you in the world. Finding your way and your dream in this life is what truly matters.

Living someone else's dream will not make you happy. Some of us spend a lifetime trying to figure out who we are and how to connect with our true selves. There are times when we have to learn the hard way, getting hurt and being disappointed, but we come away from the experience stronger and more connected to ourselves.

When you are happy and surrounded with love, including love for yourself, you are one with your spirit, you feel harmony. When you connect to your spirit, you become that spirit. When something is wrong and you feel emotionally unwell – sad or hurt, for instance – your spirit is giving you signals to change, or to notice the signs. When your spirit is suffering, you need to release these emotions, letting go of them.

One of the ways to keep your spirit healthy is by expressing your emotions through dance. Dance is an art form that helps connect you with your feelings and express them. When you do the Four Elements and Expressing Emotions exercises, for instance, your body expresses your emotions through movement: you move in whatever way you feel – in any way you are moved to move. You are letting go.

I have met many people who think they can't dance, or who say they don't feel the rhythm of the music. Many are shy to even try. Unless you are following a specific style of dance or are training to become a professional dancer, there are no rules for how to dance – every one of us can do it; we just have to let our spirits guide us. Any move you make while dancing that comes from the real you, from the way you feel, is dancing. Don't let anyone tell you otherwise. Just dance and express yourself in your own unique way.

I have worked with people who are confined to wheelchairs. They did not believe that they could ever dance. Guess what – they can! I told them, "If you can move even just one finger, you can dance. Close your eyes and see yourself dancing; move with your mind and spirit." At the end of the class, everyone was dancing in his or her own way. Their spirits were happy, the energy bringing smiles to their faces.

When you dance, feel your spirit dancing with your body. Then stop the movement of the body for a moment but let the spirit continue the dance. Even though your body is not moving, you'll feel the movement of your spirit with your mind. When we are able to connect body, mind, and spirit in dance, they become one, and this powerful life source brings new energy into our being.

ACKNOWLEDGMENTS

Special thanks to my daughter, Baiba Zandmane, for her help and encouragement.

Thanks to Peter Ross for the beautiful book design, to Gordon Hawkins and Ilze Viksnina for their evocative photographs and support, and to Charles Wong for his support and work on my website.

And finally, thanks to my editor, Judy Phillips; this book would not have been possible without your help.